I0076903

The Smart Apartment Investor: My How-To Guide for Buying and Managing Apartment Buildings for Creating and Transferring Family Wealth

Copyright © 2014-2016 by J.J. Panzer
Edited by Antonio C. White

ISBN Number: 978-0-692-68845-8
Published by Real Matters Publishing
www.RealMattersPublishing.com

AUTHOR'S NOTE

This book contains the opinions and ideas of its author. It is intended to provide helpful and informative material on the subject it addresses. It is sold with the understanding that the author/publisher are not engaged in rendering legal, financial, investment or any other kind of personal professional advice or services in the book. It is not meant to contradict, disregard, or interfere with advice any such professionals. Results not typical. No guarantees are made in this material. Invest money at your own risk. It is possible to lose money investing in real estate and apartment investing. Should you have questions or worries about investing in real estate, contact a professional property manager or real estate attorney.

What readers are saying about
"The Smart Apartment Investor" by J.J. Panzer

"With J.J.'s guidance I traded my single unit for a nine-unit apartment building with positive cash flow and long term appreciation potential. Calling J.J.'s approach 'smart' is an understatement, it's a game changer."

Amy B.

––––––––––––––

"RMC has been a real partner to us in our real estate ventures. They've not only found us great properties to buy, they have done all the financial analysis, introduced us to lenders and advised us on strategy. Once the properties were purchased they moved seamlessly into property management, where they've taken care of everything from interacting with tenants, turning around vacancies, improving tenant quality, recommending reasonable rent increases, managing standard repairs to dealing with apartment fires. We have a high level of trust in the RMC team, top to bottom. They've educated us on the business of rental property ownership."

Sincerely,
Suzi W.

––––––––––––––

"We approached JJ and the Real Management Company about renting a condominium we owned. Instead, they suggested that we consider selling the condo, using a 1031 exchange, and investing in a multi-unit property. Ker-pow! The 1031 exchange allowed us to defer taxes, sink roughly a million new dollars into TWO apartment buildings with healthy cap rates, and we found ourselves presiding over an effective TRIPLING of our investment inside of four years."

Cheers,
Doug W.

Dedication

This book is dedicated to my father for giving me a solid foundation to build upon and my mother who taught me the value of professional record keeping. Thank you to my wife, Michelle for being such an amazing support to me with this expanded vision and to our daughter Amelia whom I dream one day of teaching the family business– just as soon as she completes Potty Training.

TABLE OF CONTENTS

THE SMART APARTMENT INVESTOR

My How-To Guide for Buying and Managing Apartment Buildings for Creating and Transferring Family Wealth

BY J.J. PANZER

Introduction:

What Is the Smart Apartment Investor?

My "Aha!" moment happened when I was working as a property manager. I started out in 2002 working with my dad at the Real Management Company, the company he founded. I spent the first few years getting to know the business from the inside. I dealt with the leasing, the day-to-day management, the tenant complaints, the contractors, all of the little stuff on a daily basis that I could understand and get to know from making small individual day-to-day decisions on how the property and the relationships of operating the building would be managed. It felt like every day someone was demanding something and I wasn't sure if I could do it without getting into trouble. It felt like a trial by fire, but I had a salary and I was secure in my job. That was all I needed at the time but I wondered how I'd ever earn the kind of salary I wanted working in the family property management company.

My realization came as I rented my clients' apartments and I could clearly see their income going up every time the rent went up. For example, $250 per month in additional rent after a turnover led to $3,000 of additional income every year. They'd do that a few times in different units and after a few years they could get a new loan and take out a new loan with a higher balance and take several hundred thousand dollars to buy another building or spend on something like college tuition for their kids or a boat. I started to think, "Wow, that looks like a good deal. Maybe I should do that." I realized that a bigger salary wasn't where I'd make my money. I'd do like my clients did and save for an apartment building that would provide positive cash flow that would be equivalent to a second salary resulting from the diligent management I'd been doing for others.

To give you a little example of just what we're talking about here I'm going to show you about a building that we work with and how it's grown over the past 14 years. This is a five unit building; it's four apartments and an office and these are some of the ways that we measure the growth and success of an apartment building. We start with purchase price, gross rent per year, net operating income, Cap rate. We'll talk about these in detail a little bit more later but these are the basic measures. (See Figure 1.)

Figure 1. Wealth Building Plan for 1 building over 14 years.

Year	Purchase Price	Gross Rents	Net Operating Income	Cap Rate
1998	$850,000.00	$69,000.00	$50,000.00	5.88%
2012	$1,850,000.00	$152,280.00	$120,000.00	6.49%

In 1998 when we bought the building it was purchased for $850,000. Gross rents were $69,000, net operating income $50,000 and the cap rate was 5.88%. I did not know what the Cap rate meant at the start, but I'll explain it in a moment.

The refinance price, we just got a new loan, at a $1,850,000. That's pretty good; $1 million in equity over 14 years. $152,280 a year in rent. That's also really good. $152,000 a year in rent, so it's gone up quite drastically. Net operating income $120,000 and a cap rate of 6.49% over time. Nothing drastic, nothing special done at this building other than just making the small decisions every day that make the building profitable: collecting the rents, paying the bills, dealing with maintenance, dealing with the life stuff that happens with tenants and clients. This is what we do on a daily basis and this is what you can do to build this kind of wealth with your first investment.

Chapter 1 :
My Smart Apartment Investor
Wealth Building Plan

Buy your first apartment building Manage the building for long-term growth

Within 10 years, buy your next apartment building.

It's simple, but that does not mean it's easy. Property management is a lot of work if it's done right and when it requires your full attention it's a full-time job on top of whatever other career and family obligations you have in your life. That's why rental property owners have been paying RMC to manage for their buildings since 1980. The good news is that you can absolutely build wealth through rental property investment and I am going to show you how.

The key aspect of my wealth-building plan is leveraging the equity in your first building to purchase a second apartment building within a 10-year time frame. "Leveraging your equity" means you get to buy a second building by using the appreciation in value from the first building as your down payment for the second. You're not saving money from your job or from your cash flow on the first building to buy the second property, you're getting that money from the bank with no out of pocket cost to you.

Sounds good, doesn't it? By the time you've bought two buildings in 10 years, you are well on your way to financial success and security through your real estate investments. You can count on two successful buildings to provide cash flow, or an extra "salary" for you.

You'll notice I have up to a 10-year timetable for this plan. In my plan, we invest in the long term. This is a "get rich slow" plan, not a "get rich quick" scheme.

Getting Started: Step One, The Buying Phase

The buying phase consists of three important phases:

Part One: Focus your search

What kind of property you going to buy? How much of a down payment do you have to invest? What kinds of assets can you identify that are underutilized and can be exploited to make you money?

Part Two: Identifying and finding the right property

This process is more similar to identifying the next superstar musical talent for a record deal than simply shopping in the store. It's always possible to find a good investment but it's not easy and it can take time and effort.

Part Three: Negotiate the deal

This phase is very important and it can make or break the deal. Your real estate agent will help you make sure your questions about the property are satisfactorily answered before you close escrow and the money and building change hands.

Your first step in focusing your search is to find a good agent. Look for someone who has extensive experience and knowledge of the market in which you're searching. Someone you feel comfortable talking and working with because you're going to spend a lot of time together in person, on the phone, and over email as you go through the phases of this process.

The big question: how much are you going to be able to invest?

My best advice is to have at least 30-40% equity from day one. For example, if you're buying a building worth $2,000,000 you need to have between $600,000 and $800,000 in cash as your down payment. You can buy a decent two to four-unit apartment building in San Francisco for between $1,500,000 and $2,000,000. By investing with a 30-40% down payment you should be able to buy a property that produces positive cash flow, or your "second salary" from day one. **Don't buy a building that doesn't produce**

positive cash flow from day one. Taking care of this building is a job; you wouldn't go to work every day for free, just for the chance to "build equity" in your company. That would get old really fast, wouldn't it? The same holds true here: **don't own and manage a real estate investment without getting a return on that investment.**

Expanding Your Range

When it comes time to focus your search make sure you expand your range beyond the maximum price of a building that you could buy. For example, if you have $500,000 to invest and you want to make sure you make at least a 30% down payment the most expensive building you could buy would be $1,500,000. Even so, don't just look at buildings priced below $1,500,000 because you could find a building priced at $1,750,000 that's overpriced and has been sitting on the market for a long time. This kind of building could potentially be negotiated into your price range if you find a buyer who's willing to settle for a lower price. The smart apartment investor looks at a wide variety of possibilities to find the right one.

The Scouting Phase

Finally, once you've set your price range, you get ready to go out and visit properties in person. You're going to spend a lot of time walking through buildings so get prepare yourself and allow ample time to find a good fit. You're going to see lots of interesting spaces. Some will be well designed and others will be funky and weird. Some will be old and tired and others will be newly renovated and look sharp and attractive. This is why I use the word "scouting" instead of "shopping" or "searching." This process is strategic. Depending on the market you may never be able to see all of the properties that are available for sale before more come available and you have to start over again. In some very competitive markets there may only be a few buildings available and you may have to wait for the right opportunity to present itself to you. You never know when a property you thought was out of reach will become available. There's a lot of opportunity out there and it's your job to throw away all of the crap, to throw away all of the buildings that are no good and get started looking for that one true superstar. The Tom Brady in the 6th round of the draft, the Michael Jackson that's going to be multiplatinum for you as an apartment building investment. This plan is a comprehensive process.

Chapter 2: My Smart Apartment Secrets

Secret #1: You make your money when you buy

You make your money when you buy a building, not when you sell. This is why I recommend spending a lot of time on this process. Get comfortable with it because the better the price you get from the beginning the higher your cash flow will be and the better your "starting salary" will be with this new job you're taking on. You lock in your profit over the long run by buying well not by selling your property. The day you sell can be a good day to harvest your profits but it's also the end of your equity appreciation and your monthly salary checks from this job so *the day you sell isn't nearly as important as the day you buy.*

Be patient

This process can take you six months to a year of going out once a week or on the weekends trying to find that right building, getting to know when you walk into a "good building" as opposed to how it feels when you walk into a building that doesn't feel so good. You may miss opportunities early on; don't feel bad about that. It's part of your education in finding that right building that will make you $1,000,000 in 14 years and plenty of cash flow to support your lifestyle along the way.

Know your Market

Part of the market preparation, in addition to going out and actually looking at buildings that are for sale, is going out and understanding what neighborhoods are like. You need to know your market. If you're looking in San Francisco, you need to know: Why do people to want to live in particular neighborhoods more than others? Your customers are going to be tenants, people with good jobs who are going to want to live in your building. Where are they working and how easy is it for them to get to work every day?

Another crucial part of your education is to know the market rates for apartments in the markets in which you're interested in buying an apartment building. Take a look at apartment listings online to see what kinds of rents people are asking for different kinds of apartments. Take note of the amenities that are included in one apartment that makes it more expensive than another. For example, an apartment with laundry in the unit and a garage parking space is going to rent for more than one in a building with coin operated laundry and no parking or a Laundromat at the end of the block. Tenants pay more for apartments that offer those amenities and conveniences. One of the things I like to do, and this is probably just because I'm an apartment investment nerd and I get a kick out of this, is visit apartment open houses. I go to a neighborhood that I'm interested in, have coffee, have brunch and then follow those A-frame signs that the agents put out for homes and condos and buildings for sale or apartments for rent. Clearly I'm not going to be renting anything but as an investor it's great to get a feeling for how other people see the market. Take advantage of other people's knowledge and experience and get a feeling for what they think their apartments are worth. Spend some time, be patient, get to know your market well.

This is not a speculative game. You will make money if you buy and manage your building well. If a building is overpriced this is typically because the seller either doesn't understand the market or knows the property has untapped potential and wants to sell you potential instead of reliable income. For example, if seller has apartments that are renting for two thirds of the maximum potential market rent it doesn't make sense for the property to be priced as if the units are earning that maximum potential market rent. Even if all a buyer would have to do is raise the rents with a rent increase notice this is a property management strategy that adds value to the building. Without completing this rent increase process the building is worth what it produces with tenants paying two thirds of market rent, not full market rent. The seller cannot expect to earn top dollar and you should not be willing to pay top dollar for this building. Validate the rents as they currently stand, don't speculate on what the rents could possibly be.

Secret #2: Validate, Don't Speculate!

Let's say you've done your homework, you know what market rents are in the area where you're shopping and you are comparing two different buildings. You've visited them both, you've seen the units and examined the rents. One building has several units with tenants who are still under lease and who moved in less than a year ago and their rents are higher than you've seen similar units get in the same area. The other building has several units with tenants who are still under lease and who moved in less than a year ago and their rents are lower than you've seen similar units get in the same area. Which building should you consider buying? Let's compare. If you buy the building with the above-market rents and you pay a reasonable price for that building based on the above-market rents you could be in trouble when the leases expire and the tenants move out, especially if you have trouble getting that same rent once again. Your income will drop, your mortgage and other expenses stay the same and, as a result, your profit shrinks. This means you just took a pay cut from your investment, your "second job" as an apartment investor, and things are tight.

If you buy the second building, the one with the below-market rents, and you pay a reasonable price based on these actual rents, you could find yourself in a good position as the units turn over. If you're able to increase your rents to what you know the market will bear then your income increases while the rest of your expenses stay the same. As a result you get a pay increase from your investment, your "second job" as an apartment investor, and you're enjoying better cash flow and improved property value.

"Validate, don't speculate!" means to look for buildings where you're confident you can make a decent profit with the current income in place. This means a building has to pay you a sufficient "second salary" without any "ifs" such as, "If I can increase my rents by $200 per month, then I'll make the net income I want."

Looking at income and expenses

How do you get information on income and expenses? It's easy: sellers are required to disclose income and expenses to you as part of the "disclosure package" that is made available as a part of the sale. This disclosure package will include a "rent roll," or a list of all of the current apartments, the names of the tenants, the date they moved in to the building, how much they paid in security deposits when they moved in, and any other charges the tenants pay to the landlord every month. This is your income. This is why the building has any value at all, because of these agreements that tenants will pay to live in the property. **Apartment buildings aren't houses. Their value is not based solely on what other people will pay to buy them.** This is certainly part of the equation but it's deeper than that. The value of apartment buildings is also based on how the rents a building owner could collect and the expenses they'll have to pay to collect those rents.

A building that has below-market rents harbors an opportunity to take advantage of the potential to increase rents to market. Nevertheless, **a Smart Apartment Investor won't pay more for the building than the value of its current rents just to get access to this opportunity.** A Smart Apartment Investor buys a building based on the value of current rents and then captures the increase in value as their reward for being smart and applying skill and hard work to create a successful investment.

Seeing what's possible

Economizing on expenses is a great way to increase your return on investment without increasing rents. For example, if you see in the disclosure package that the current owner is paying for trash service that comes every day but the trash cans aren't full every day you can talk to the garbage company and have them tell you the recommended service level for a building of that size. It's not in their best interest to pro-actively offer their customers less service but if you ask them they'll tell you you can get by with less frequent service, thereby saving yourself on this expense. A penny saved is a penny earned! I have done this for my own properties and for my clients and it's a great strategy for increasing your net income. As a property manager I have access to my clients' expense records showing what it cost to operate their buildings. Without compromising my clients' confidentiality, I can use this data to accurately project how much an eight-unit apartment building should pay for trash service, insurance, or any other expense and recognize these inconsistencies in buildings being offered for sale. Conversely, sometimes a seller or their agent can under-report certain expenses thereby making their building seem more profitable than it really is.

Once you get your income and expenses, you can calculate your net operating income.

Calculating Net Operating Income (NOI):

Gross potential rent
- Vacancy factor of 2-5%
= Effective rental income
- Operating Expenses
= Net Operating Income (NOI)

This is a crucial detail for evaluating pricing and profitability of an apartment building investment. Begin by taking your **Gross Scheduled Rent**, or all rents that are due to be paid each month plus a reasonable guess at market rent for any vacant units, and multiply this by 12 months. A **Vacancy Factor** helps you anticipate turnover costs. **Turnover** is when your tenants move out and you go through the process of replacing them. To discover your Vacancy Factor, subtract a vacancy factor of two to five percent. This represents the cost of having a unit vacant between tenants. If you're confident in your ability to find new tenants and generate market rents quickly then go with the lower end of the spectrum, two percent; **if you're new and want to make sure you'll still make money even if a vacancy takes a little longer to rent then go with the five percent vacancy factor.** Gross scheduled rent minus Vacancy Factor gives you your **Effective Rental Income.** Next you deduct all of your operating expenses, those cash expenses that are required to operate the building effectively and command market rents. Operating expenses include property taxes, insurance, property management fees, utilities, janitorial service, and the like. Effective rental income minus operating expenses equals *Net Operating Income* or NOI.

Let's figure out what your profit will be from your apartment building investment. NOI is what you're going to use to pay the mortgage every month because you're not going to buy a building with 100% cash. We'll discuss why later on, but suffice to say that buying buildings with all cash isn't a tool in a Smart Apartment Investor's toolbox.

To figure out what your profit is going to be each month you have to find out how much it's going to cost to borrow the rest of your capital. Get a referral to a loan broker or a banker who makes commercial and residential loans. Get a sense of market interest rates for the amount you're looking to borrow and go online to find a loan amortization calculator. Entering your loan amount, a reasonable market interest rate, and setting it for a fully amortized 30-year loan will give you the amount of your monthly payment. If you subtract this from your monthly NOI you'll see if the investment will be cash flow positive from day one, whether it'll pay you a "second salary" or it'll cost you money.

Never buy a building that doesn't make some money from day one. Some people reason that the building will grow in value in a few years because market prices are increasing so they'll tolerate a break-even investment. This is not how a Smart Apartment Investor buys a building.

Two more important tools for analyzing an apartment building's return on investment and pricing are the capitalization rate and gross rent multiplier. *Capitalization Rate*, or "cap rate" is essentially the return on investment you'd get if you bought the building with all cash. As Smart Apartment Investors we don't buy buildings with all cash, but it's important to know that Cap Rates tell you the building's ability to pay for itself by returning your initial capital investment to you over time. The formula for capitalization rate is simply net operating income divided by purchase price. **A higher cap rate means you have a higher net operating income or a lower purchase price. A lower cap rate means lower net operating income or higher purchase price.** Cap rates can vary from a negative number to ten percent or more. The higher your cap rate the better a job you did buying and operating your building. As you increase your income or eliminate your expenses you can increase your cap rate because your purchase price stays the same. Your cap rate considers your expenses so it's a good measure of profitability. You want to buy buildings at a higher cap rate but be sure to examine income and expense numbers thoroughly to make sure they're represented reasonably before you accept that a building with a higher cap rate is a better opportunity to buy. For example, if an expense has been under-reported in the disclosure package this means that NOI is higher and therefore cap rates are higher. When you buy this building you could find that you need to spend more for this under-reported expense and you'll have a lower NOI and a lower cap rate.

Understanding the Gross Rent Multiplier

The **Gross Rent Multiplier** (GRM) is simply the purchase price divided by the gross scheduled rents. It doesn't speak directly to your return on investment but rather gives you an easy way to compare one building to another with regard to price and its relation to gross income. GRM doesn't consider expenses so it's not a measure of profitability. **You typically want to buy a building with a lower GRM because that means it's priced lower.**

It takes time to get good at looking at these numbers and calculating cap rates, GRMs, and understanding NOI. The more buildings you analyze the better you'll get at recognizing something fishy in the numbers. You'll say,

"Well, that cap rate looks a little funky. Why would anyone price their building as a 12% cap rate in a market where properties are routinely selling at 6% cap rates?" If you see this, dig into the numbers and visit the property to find out why it's priced so low.

Making an Offer

Now we've covered focusing and the scouting process. Once you've worked the numbers and you think you've found a building you want to buy you have to decide if you want to proceed. Here's where the negotiations start. It's time to make an offer.

Don't be afraid to make an offer

On one hand, making an offer is a big deal but on the other hand, it's really not. It's a big deal because you're telling someone, "I want to buy your property" and you're required to put down a deposit of around 3% of the offering price to show you mean it. If you don't perform you could lose your deposit! It's not such a big deal because you can insert contingencies into your contract that allow you to cancel the contract before it goes through and recover your deposit. Your agent will recommend that you put contingencies in your contract related to the condition of the property (an inspection contingency), a contingency related to your ability to obtain financing at specified terms (a financing contingency), or that it appraises at a specified price (an appraisal contingency). Any of these conditions gives you the opportunity to back out of the deal and cancel the contract if you find that the property isn't what you'd hoped or you are otherwise unable or unwilling to complete the deal.

Understanding Contingencies

My favorite way to think of contingencies is with this example: let's imagine you pull out a piece of paper and you write on the paper right now, "I hereby promise in this legally binding contract to give one million dollars to J.J. Panzer of the Real Management Company next Friday" and then you sign it at the bottom and have it notarized. You've just promised to give me one million dollars! Thanks! Would you do that? Probably not. Now, if you amend the contract before you sign it and write, "Unless I change my mind," at the very end. How would you feel about signing that? Pretty good, right? All week long you'll tell me, "I'm going to pay you that million dollars on Friday" and then when Friday rolls around you say, "Never mind. I changed my mind." That's essentially how the purchase contract works. You promise to pay a specified price until a certain time and you're free to change your mind at any point up until that time arrives.

Types of Contract Contingencies

There are myriad contingencies in a purchase contract, but your inspection contingency is one of the most important. For me, inspecting an apartment building is a bit like a nature walk. Imagine you're walking through the woods and you find some mushrooms that look pretty good. Are you going to eat them? Unless you're a Mycologist and you have extensive knowledge of what kinds of mushrooms are safe to eat you're not likely to take this chance. An inspection period is like being on a nature accompanied by the Park Ranger who knows everything about the forest, in applying this idea to a property inspection, the general contractor or a structural engineer is like the knowledgeable Park Ranger and when it comes to understanding what makes a structurally sound property, these experts can help you to determine everything from whether dry rot on stairs or a stain on the ceiling could be indicative of an expensive problem or an issue that's simpler to fix. These experts are there to guide you in making sure you don't get sick from investing in a poisonous property.

The Inspection Contingency

Obviously you don't know everything you need to know based on visiting it during an open house. If your seller accepts your inspection contingency you will have a specified amount of time during which you can gain access to every square inch of the property and bring professional inspectors, contractors, engineers, and other professionals to render an opinion on the quality of the property. For example, if you see an exterior stairway with some dry rot or other damage you can get an estimate of the cost required to repair it. If you feel it's a small number you can accept it and decide if you want to repair it when you own the property. If it's a bigger number you can decide to try to renegotiate the price of the property downward to compensate for the cost of repairing it later. You won't usually ask the seller to fix something larger before you close escrow but for smaller items that's also an option. Finally, if the problem is too large and you don't want to deal with it, you can change your mind and cancel the contract. Your agent will help you through this process and advise you how to handle conditions that present themselves in your inspections.

Getting a General Contractors Inspection

Most concerns about the condition of the building can be addressed by obtaining a general contractor's inspection.

This is a standard part of inspecting a building and can cost between a few hundred to over one thousand dollars. For your money you'll get a full written report that could be as much as 15 or 20 pages and suggestions of other important experts who should be called to render their opinions on the systems of the building. For example, you might need to contact a roofer, a plumber to inspect a boiler or other central heat system, a structural engineer to inspect the foundation, or an electrician to tell you whether the building's power service is adequate and the system is in good condition.

One good example of something you might find when you're inspecting a new property occurred in a building I bought a few years ago. The seller disclosed to us that the electrical system in the building was obsolete. The circuit breakers were installed in the 1970s and were made by a company that had gone out of business because their product was faulty and had been implicated in a number of fires. The question was whether this was like that forest mushroom that might poison me and make me cancel the deal so I brought in my electrician for a proposal to replace the electrical system. His proposal was $25,000 so we decided we could budget that into our purchase price because we knew the seller wouldn't give us a credit. We could live with it because the purchase price was good enough to allow us to fix the problem immediately when we closed escrow.

Staying Focused Throughout the Process

Remember to stay focused throughout this process from beginning to end. Your focus is to get the deal and start building your wealth as a Smart Apartment Investor. Don't let one small detail derail your deal. A lot of times the back and forth of a negotiation process and contract involves your saying, "Mr. Seller, I went up on the roof and your roof is 20 years old and it's got moss growing on it and it's in really bad shape and you are responsible for your roof. I'm not buying your building unless you give me a $25,000 credit to replace that roof." Go ahead and make that request if your agent tells you there could be some room to negotiate. Don't stick too hard to your $25,000 number. If you get $15,000 or even $10,000 it's better than nothing. Your focus is to get the building. The Smart Apartment Investor doesn't let a $25,000 credit request derail an otherwise acceptable deal.

Now think about the example at the beginning of this book. Our example property had one million dollars in equity appreciation over 14 years, during which time the owner collected a "second salary" through positive cash flow. That's a good investment and the picture doesn't change dramatically if you pay a little bit more at the beginning or have to invest $25,000 in a roof two years after you buy the building. Don't let the small parts of the negotiation derail you as you go through the process. Stay on target, get the deal because it's worth making the investment. If the building made sense at the original price, it'll still make sense for you if you didn't get the $25,000 credit from the seller.

Chapter 3: So Now You've Done It, You're a Landlord! What's next?

You've navigated the negotiations, removed your contingencies and the money and property have changed hands. Get set for a decade of being a landlord and property manager. Welcome to the club! You own a building, you have responsibilities and it's time for you to manage for growth, control and minimize liabilities, maximize and exploit opportunities. Take good care of your building and it'll take good care of you. In this section we're going to discuss the importance of tenant management, vendors, government regulation, and record keeping.

Tenant Management: It's About Relationships

The most important part of managing for growth is taking care of your tenants so they'll keep paying you rent. Tenants are the lifeblood of your business. Without tenants you've got an empty building that costs you money every month and produces no income. That's not good, no "second salary" for you! You need your tenants, even when they're making maintenance requests or even missing their rent payments and it feels like all they do is cost you money and waste your time. They're still integral to your success. Handling these challenges is where you earn your money. In this section we are going to discuss the people management vs. property management, how to effectively handle rent collection (an always tricky and challenging process), and how to lease your units effectively.

People Management vs. Property Management

My father has always said that "property management" is an inaccurate name for the work we do. Yes, managing apartment buildings is work but the truth is that properties themselves don't change too much over time. Things break, systems wear out, disasters happen, and we're there to handle all of those circumstances but the more intensive part of this job is managing the relationships with the tenants. The relationship is a fascinating one. The landlord-tenant relationship is one where the tenant gets up every morning and spends a third or more of their day working, probably doing something don't greatly enjoy and they get a paycheck every two weeks. Then they take a third or more of that paycheck they've worked so hard to earn and they write the landlord a big check to pay for the largest living expense in their budget. You have a big responsibility to take good care of these people so they'll keep working every day to give you a big chunk of the money they earn. Keep this perspective even when it gets contentious, annoying, or stressful and it will help you make good decisions.

Relationships, remember as you are a property owner, yes you are operating a business, yes you must make money, but you are providing a fundamental human right; food, water, shelter the three big things a human being needs to thrive. You are providing something that people need, so your role is to take good care of the people who live in your property. What is their role? To live there and pay you, to go to work every day and give you a third of their money that they spend a third of their life making. Their role is to be there and to watch for things. To tell you when there is something wrong. To take care of the building, to be your eyes and ears because they see it every day and you don't. You really don't have to inspect your building every day, your tenants should do that, they should see things for you. They should alert you to what is going on.

Finally, don't get emotional and try not to take things personally. Your tenants rarely set out to antagonize you deliberately. I've seen that circumstance, it does happen, but in my experience the more likely explanation for difficult behavior is carelessness or misunderstanding.

Collections - An Essential Task

Many people are afraid of asking people for money. It can be scary but this is your job now. Get the money. Be serious about collections. You have to be firm and disciplined about this. When your rent due date rolls around and someone still hasn't paid you will develop a standard operating procedure to go collect that money or take the appropriate actions to start an eviction. It's one of the least pleasant parts of being a property manager but it's absolutely essential. I've met clients who have spent a year chasing their tenants for rent without effectively collecting it and it's one of the reasons why many people hire a professional property manager. They just don't want to face it.

You might not believe it but your reliable, consistent rent collection procedures and behavior are a benefit to your tenants, even if they haven't paid the rent. A perfect example of this was a client who came to me saying she hadn't collected rent from her tenant in over a year. I didn't manage her property yet but she was at her wits' end and couldn't figure out how to get the rent paid. The first time the tenant didn't pay the rent my client called her and asked her where the money was. Her tenant started crying and explained that she was pregnant and the baby was due any day but wasn't doing so great and her husband had gotten hurt and was disabled and unable to work. A terrible situation, right? My client was overwhelmed with sympathy for her tenant because of her story so when the tenant asked my client to give her a little bit more time to pay the rent my client, of course, agreed.

Month two rolled around and my client was 30 days behind in collecting the rent. When the rent didn't come in the next month my client delegated the rent collection to her husband because she thought he'd have more success doing it. He was even more scared about collecting the rent from her so he didn't try to push her to pay, he simply wished her well. My client never followed up with her husband nor the tenant so here we were, over a year later and no rent had been paid.

When I started working with this client and her husband I called the tenant and introduced myself to her. I expected her to become defensive, avoid talking to me, or be evasive. She hadn't paid rent for a year and my sole purpose was to go get the rent for my clients, right? Well, she was very cordial and when I asked her if I could come visit and inspect her apartment she gladly agreed! I went for my inspection and met the tenant as agreed and I could tell she and her family had had a very difficult year. The house was a disaster, filthy and disorganized and close to uninhabitable. Nevertheless the tenant doesn't seem to be aware that I'm there because a year's rent is due. I sit down with her and gently ask her about her relationship with her landlords. She starts telling me how great her landlord is and I am thinking, "Yeah, I'd love my landlord, too, if she didn't collect any rent from me for a year!" I couldn't dance around the issue any longer: I asked her if she knew how her landlords, these people she liked so much, felt not having received rent for a full year.

The tenant's jaw dropped and she was speechless. I had been wondering how she could be so out of touch with reality and then I got my explanation. When the landlord first called and she was pregnant and her baby was sick and her husband was disabled, it was right before she went into the hospital for a very difficult delivery. She admitted to having had trouble with her finances after the baby was born, though it seemed like she wasn't that good at keeping track of her finances before that, either. She then went on to explain to me that she'd entrusted her checkbook and all of her money to a cousin who had taken charge of balancing the checkbook and sending out the rent each month. She completely thought the rent was being paid because the rent was coming out of the account and the checks were clearing. It was just that it never arrived in the landlord's hands...for a year! Her "trusted cousin" had been stealing the rent money from her for a year! The cousin had probably only figured she'd get a month or two before someone figured it out but the gravy train kept rolling for a year!

The saddest part is that if the landlord had been more on top of her business and served a three-day notice after the rent went unpaid the first month her tenant would have had a chance to recover. The tenant would have realized it immediately, perhaps she'd have dealt with her thieving cousin and gotten her money back, and the whole problem would have been averted. The landlord's failure to serve the notice turned out to have failed the tenant and put her in a position from which she couldn't recover. When the tenant realized what was going on she asked for a few weeks to clear out her family and their possessions and voluntarily surrendered the premises to us.

The moral of this story is that you have to be reliable and professional in collecting your rent. Don't spend a lot of your time and energy chasing your tenants with phone calls, emails, or personal visits to ask for the rent. Serve a three-day notice to pay rent or quit as your way of opening the dialog. Now your tenant is on the clock, and if they don't pay in time then you have the right to file for an unlawful detainer and regain possession of your unit so you can rent it to someone else and get the money coming in again. In the rental business you aren't selling a physical product, you're selling time spent in a specific space. If your tenant doesn't pay their rent on time it's the same as any other situation where someone doesn't pay for something that they're taking from you. Starting the legal process reserves your rights.

Leasing - Go Get Yourself a Raise!

Leasing is time-consuming and labor-intensive but it's imperative to do it well because it's the best way to increase your income and avoid wasting time and money in the future. In this section we're going to discuss several important topics related to leasing. First, we'll discuss the importance of taking your time through the process, then we'll talk about developing and using your knowledge of the rental market, then we'll talk about pricing strategies and, finally, we'll talk about the tenant screening process.

Don't Be in a Rush to Lease Your Apartments!

I have clients who panic when they get a 30-day notice to vacate from one of their tenants. They're scared to be without rent for a few weeks or a month and they're afraid of the cost of renovating the unit to get it ready for a new tenant. All of these unknowns! They're afraid the vacancy cost and unit turnover expenses will break them. When I get a vacancy notice I see it as an opportunity to go get a better rent and make some money in the long run. The opportunity to try for a higher rent outweighs the vacancy and renovation cost because higher rent lasts for a year or more and the pain of a vacancy is temporary. Don't rush through turnovers. It's important to stay focused on the big picture of increasing income and reducing expenses.

Smart Apartment Investors understand that the most important time they spend with their tenants is when they first meet them, screen them, and move them into the building. This is the time you'll be able to set the tone on the relationship, teach them how you want to frame your communications, and that you want to work together. It'll save you so much time in the long run if you just slow down and make sure you cover all of the details we're going to discuss next.

Maintaining Your Market Knowledge

You learned a little bit about the rental market in your neighborhood earlier when you were scouting for buildings and evaluating the property. Regardless of your building's size you're probably not going to have very many vacancies throughout the course of a typical year. If you can increase the rents you want more vacancies but if you've got a building full of market-rate tenants you probably don't want too many vacancies, especially not at once. Hopefully the whole building doesn't go vacant at the same time. That would be a problem! Each time you have a new vacancy your market knowledge is going to be, at best, a few months old and rather out-of-date. It's going to take a whole new process of searching on Craig's List, visiting open houses, and researching currently vacant units to get back up to speed. As we said above, don't rush this process, especially in the beginning.

Your tenant's 30 day notice to vacate is your warning that they're going to stop paying the rent and you need to ramp up your market knowledge. Go learn how much the rents have changed in your neighborhood. Start by going to Craigslist.com and view comparable units by sorting from low to high price and you'll get a feeling for the range of prices you could offer. Look through the postings and make pretend that you are a tenant. If you needed to rent an apartment would your unit be more or less attractive than the others in the same price range? Think about whether you can distinguish your unit from others by adding amenities, sprucing your unit up a bit by repainting, changing or upgrading the flooring, or completely remodeling the apartment. If you are considering upgrading or remodeling you might even want to ask your tenant for permission to enter and get some bids before they move out so you can decide before the unit is empty and stops producing income for you.

Pricing Strategies for Effective Leasing

Once you've established the proper range for your unit within a $300-500 window it's time to pick a price. When it's clean and ready to rent I put it on the market at the highest price I can realistically imagine getting for it. I strongly prefer to start out high and bring the price down than to price it lower and collect a dozen applications on day one. Whenever I get multiple applications for a unit right away I'm concerned that I left money on the table. I get "seller's remorse!" I prefer to overprice my units a little bit and get no response or disinterested responses from tenants at first. This way when I reduce the price and start to get better responses and collecting applications I feel pretty confident I didn't leave any money on the table.

Starting at a high price also gives you a chance to learn more about your market. If you get disinterested responses from tenants go ahead and ask them what else they've seen on the market and what they'd need to make this apartment work at your price. If they need a place with parking and you don't have parking in your building there's not much you can do. If you start hearing that the unit is dark or they don't like the carpet you might be able to do something with that feedback.

Throughout this marketing process try your best to focus on the positive, your opportunity to increase your income, not the negative the time you're spending showing the unit and the money you're losing while the unit is vacant. I promise that you'll find a good balance between long vacancy times and seller's remorse the more you develop your skills and experience the thrill of getting good tenants at good rents.

Tenant Screening

Bingo! After a few weeks of open houses and posting ads on Craigslist.com you've finally gotten a rental application and it looks pretty good. Congratulations! Don't rush. Be careful. It's time to screen the prospective tenant or tenants to make sure they are going to be ready, willing, and able to pay your rent. The pain of a vacancy is nothing compared to the agony of going through an eviction immediately after the tenant moves in! Remember that you're extending credit to your tenant by allowing them to occupy your property based on a promise to pay rent in the future.

Your screening criteria should include:

- verification of employment
- a full credit report
- a reference from a prior landlord.

Employment Verification

When examining a tenant's employment, you want to make sure they make three times the monthly rent in gross income among all adults who will occupy your unit. Tenants who make less than three times the rent in gross income each month will find themselves in a difficult situation when the rent comes due each month: do they pay the rent or do they buy food? Examine your prospective tenants' paystubs, offer letters, and call their supervisors at work. Make sure they haven't lost their jobs recently and they're doing well at work. Verifying a prospective tenant's employment is not the same as offering to pay a year's rent up front or showing you a bank statement with $100,000 in cash. These common requests don't provide enough security for me. A bank account full of cash can be gone in an instant and prepaid rent doesn't guarantee you won't have to evict them after the pre-payment runs out.

Running a Credit Report

Next thing run a credit report. I can't tell you how many tenants walk in and say well can I give you a copy of mine? Why don't I want a copy of theirs? Because a monkey with Photoshop can easily falsify a credit report so it's essential to obtain your own copy from a credit bureau. Your local apartment association can probably direct you to a vendor that can provide these for you when you need them. I am looking for a FICO score of at least 640. This establishes that the tenant has a history, a demonstrated ability and willingness, of paying their bills on time. If you find a tenant with lots of income but bad credit, take a close look at why their score is bad. If they have lots of different accounts that are unpaid, currently and in the recent past, then they're probably disorganized or maybe they just don't like paying their bills. I don't want to rent my apartments to someone like that.

Get a Landlord Reference, but be Alert!

Getting a good landlord reference can be a problem sometimes but be careful about relaxing this requirement to get your unit rented. There's nothing quite like having a prior landlord tell you how wonderful this tenant was to make you feel good about proceeding with to writing a lease for a prospective tenant. You want to ask the prior landlord to verify some important details about the tenant's reported relationship with their former landlord: the dates they moved in and vacated the unit, the rent they paid, how much of their security deposit the landlord returned to their tenant, how many times the rent was paid late, how many times the landlord experienced behavior complaints from other tenants about this individual. All of these questions will help you verify that this person will be a good risk to move into your building. Notice we haven't discussed current landlords. Frequently tenants don't bother to put prior landlords' contact information on their rental applications leaving me with only a current landlord. I never call a current landlord. Why not? I don't call current landlords because current landlords have every incentive to lie when giving a tenancy reference. For example, if the tenant has been great and the current landlord isn't enthusiastic about losing the tenant and having to find a new one the current landlord has an incentive to tell you how bad they've been, thereby frustrating the tenant's efforts to move. If the tenant has been terrible and the landlord cannot wait to get rid of their tenant then the current landlord will have every incentive to tell you how great this tenant has been, thereby unloading a problem tenant on you!

Vendors - A Source of Value, Not Cost

Having good vendors to service your investment property makes you money. Yes, you pay them money but good vendors deliver greater value than the money they cost you. Good vendors are integral to helping to manage risk and ensure that your tenants will keep paying rent or that new tenants will pay you more rent when your units turn over. Respect your plumber, electrician, general contractor, even your janitor and garbage collector because you can't operate your building and make money without their loyal reliable service. In this section we're going to discuss how to budget for repairs and maintenance, picking a good team to help you, ensuring top-quality results for the money you invest, and ensuring quality customer service by scheduling effectively and responsibly.

Budgeting to Avoid Big, Ugly Surprises

Remember that buildings sometimes require large investments of cash. In this way, your "second salary" from your apartment building investment is very different from your salary at work. Your boss probably doesn't come to you to ask you for $25,000 to replace the roof on your office, but your apartment building will! After buying your building well and setting yourself up to make a profit every month, **make sure that you keep good reserves on hand so that you can have cash on hand for upgrades or unexpected expenses.** If you see that the paint on the outside of the building is starting to look worn and you anticipate that it'll need a paint job soon, start saving before it becomes urgent. Give yourself a year or two to save a bit here and there and prepare for the expense. Don't spend all of your "second salary" every month, keep some in the bank. **In the beginning, I recommend that a new property owner keep at least three to six months' worth of gross rental income on hand in cash.**

Smart Renovation Projects

Another important budgeting detail is to make sure you don't overspend on remodeling projects. The rental housing business is not Better Homes & Gardens. Decorate with neutral colors and finishes instead of big, bold touches so the unit will be as attractive as possible to as many people as possible. Big, bold touches are more likely to turn off potential tenants than make them fall in love. I still remember a client who told me about her experience renting the units in her 35-unit building in an upscale neighborhood. In the beginning she was wide-eyed and hopeful about how much everybody would love her apartments. She prided herself on having a great eye for details and decorations so she bought expensive chintz curtains and white carpet, spent extra on perfectly color-coordinated paint schemes and fancy details. After a while she found that prospective tenants would say things like, "Gee, I like this apartment but I don't like the curtains" or "I'm not crazy about this paint color. I'd rent it if it were a different color." Even when she rented an apartment she was very disappointed when the tenants didn't appreciate the finishes nearly as much as she did, when the curtains came back stained and damaged. It was expensive and it didn't get her any more money. **Don't decorate as if you're going to live there, renovate to make it neutral and easy to repair and replace.**

Be Wise: Amortize

Finally, as you prepare for these large expenses, be wise: amortize. Think about this as a long-term investment. Don't cut corners on your renovations. When it comes time to do a major upgrade on your building admit that it must be done, go get your bids, choose a vendor, do the job, and be glad when you get the project out of the way. Say to yourself, "Well, now that the roof is new I'm glad I won't have to think about it again for a long time." Yes, it's good to have the roofer come back every three to five years to check it and do some maintenance but you can easily prepare for that. This is an opportunity for me to put that behind me and know that that roof is in good shape."

Assembling Your Vendor Team

A good team of vendors is essential to your success over the course of the next ten years. Properly executed maintenance projects will reduce risk, ensure long-term profitability, and help you when it's time to go buy your second building. Pay close attention to the vendors you choose to work at the building. No matter what happens you must understand that you are primarily responsible for everything that happens to the building. If you choose to do your own electrical repairs to save money and you cause a fire that injures or kills someone you're clearly responsible.

Nevertheless, if you hire a bad electrician who does a bad job that causes a fire and injures or kills someone you're just as responsible. Be careful whom you pick to work on your team.

Beware of the lowest priced bidder

Be careful selecting the lowest-priced bidder because that person could get you into serious trouble. Keep an eye on value, not just price. A more expensive contractor could give you the peace of mind to know that they're going to do a good job and that you'll be happy with the result, and you won't have to go back and do it again.

After identifying your team of reliable, reasonable licensed contractors including a plumber, electrician, general contractor, roofer, and others the next most important person in your list of vendors is a good handyman. Your handyman should be a person with a broad base of skills. They'll likely have a deeper base of knowledge in one or two specific areas but they simply need to have the confidence to try a few things and the wisdom to know when to stop and tell you to call in one of the licensed contractors listed above. Your handyman can do some painting, carpentry, basic electrical work, and plumbing like changing a light switch or a faucet washer.

None of these jobs require a permit or a license to complete and a handyman can typically do them faster and for less than a licensed contractor can. At the very least your handyman can evaluate the situation, send you a photo, and help you decide which licensed vendor can complete the job. Many property owners do their own handyman work. This can help you to keep an eye on what's going on at the building because it's likely to keep you making regular visits to the property. Just be careful that you don't get in over your head or make mistakes that could cost you more in the long run or expose you to unnecessary liability.

Avoid having tenants connect directly with your vendors

You may be tempted to save yourself some time by putting your tenants directly in touch with your vendors. I see this fairly frequently when a client hires RMC after self-managing their building for a long time. Avoid this mistake because it leaves you vulnerable to repeated requests that cost you money and potentially missing developing maintenance problems as they present themselves. One example involved a client whose tenants called a handyman to fix the same window that seemed to come out of alignment every six months or so. Every time the tenant, the handyman would go out, find that the window didn't lock, and he'd shave the window a little bit to make it fit. The owner looked at the invoices, thought they looked reasonable, and paid them. After a couple of years of this the handyman found that he didn't have any window frame left to shave! After reporting this to the owner they found that the cause of the problem wasn't the window but the foundation! The wall was moving, not the window, and the handyman didn't catch this at all. By the time they figured it out the foundation couldn't be salvaged, it had to be replaced. If the owner had received the same maintenance request repeatedly maybe he'd have called his general contractor who would have caught the problem earlier.

Assuring Quality Results from your Vendor Team

As you work with your team of vendors pay close attention to be sure that the work they do is good. Nothing is automatic, you will be vetting these vendors every day. Inspect their work the first few times you hire them so you can establish that they're finished, that the work is of satisfactory quality, and if all is well, you're ready to pay their invoice. If you pay the bill before you've inspected and the job's not complete or unsatisfactory you're likely to have a harder time getting them to return and finish or correct the problem. After you've come to trust your vendors you can relax a little bit but in the beginning you have to put in the effort to make sure they're good.

Respond Quickly and Professional to Maintenance Requests

Responding to maintenance requests and delivering good quality work is how you make money. If your vendors don't respond or perform good quality work you're going to have problems with your tenants. If habitability problems pop up and they go unheeded your tenants may withhold rent to complete repairs on their own, which rarely results in satisfactory work and reasonable prices, or your tenants could even sue you for renting them an uninhabitable apartment! By providing good service your vendors make it legal for you to collect your rent. Be wary of using unlicensed friends and family members who do a little bit of locksmith work or painting as a side job. Any money you save could end up costing you big time in the end. If you've got a contractor who gives you a great rate but doesn't show up or doesn't do a good job, then the rate is really not that great. Focus on value, not simply price. Value is where of good quality and good price meet.

Get Competitive Bids

Competitive bidding is essential to operating your building profitable. You probably won't be able to bid for every kitchen faucet replacement job or light fixture that needs to be replaced but look for opportunities to challenge your preferred vendors to stay competitive by comparing their prices to other qualified vendors. When it comes to projects I rarely hand the job to my favorite plumber and accept his bid without getting at least one competitive bid. Yes, this takes extra time and effort but it's a valuable investment of time and effort. If your plumber gets the feeling maybe you're not having other bids on your projects perhaps he won't be as aggressive with pricing after he gains your business initially. You should open up your bidding process to other vendors periodically, every year or two, just to keep your preferred vendors from hiking their prices on you.

Scheduling and Customer Service

When your tenants call to request service don't promise them an immediate response. Even if you're pretty sure you can deliver a good result immediately, give yourself and your team an ample response time frame and try to under-promise and over-deliver. It's far better to promise that you'll get to the maintenance request in 48 hours and give your tenant a pleasant surprise by having someone there first thing the next morning than to promise you'll have someone there in the morning and not get to it for 48 hours. Your maintenance issues must be dealt with promptly and effectively. Give yourself hurdles that are easy to reach. "Oh yes, we'll get someone there as soon as possible, and I'll call you back to tell you approximately when." The contractor says they'll be there by Thursday; tell the tenant they'll be there by Friday. This is one good way to keep your tenants happy so they will continue to pay the rent gladly and take good care of your building.

Make sure that your vendors give you excellent service on an excellent basis. If you start to feel like, gee, your plumber came out and gave you a recommendation that in addition to the faucet you also replace the other thing in the apartment. When you said, "No," he kind of stopped answering your phone calls, and he didn't pick up the phone when you called. It started to get a little difficult. Don't be shy about going to find another plumber who will treat you better, even though that requires extra time and effort. Once again, when working with a new vendor take extra time to inspect the job before you pay the bill. Make sure that you have the vendor on-track through the entire project and that you've held back payment to make sure that the job gets done right.

Regulations - Know The Rules of the Road

In this section we're going to talk about how to operate rental housing successfully while staying up to date on regulations and legal constraints. The rental housing industry is one of the most regulated industries in the country because we provide shelter, an essential resource for everyone. This is especially important in rent-controlled jurisdictions like San Francisco. Housing is in extremely limited supply and demand is high so prices are high and competition is fierce. It can be very profitable but it's also highly regulated. A healthy attitude toward this regulation is key for maintaining your sanity and perspective in this business.

Develop your knowledge of the laws, get comfortable operating within them, and keep your knowledge up to date. I promise you'll never be bored operating rental housing. You will learn something new every day. Join a local rental housing association and subscribe to their magazine. Attend their meetings and talk to other rental property owners. I promise they'll be glad to share their knowledge and experience with you and the time you invest in making yourself a better property manager will pay dividends in the long run by helping you avoid problems and find creative solutions. Many local rental housing associations offer courses in managing rental housing geared specifically toward owner-operators and staff at property management companies. Look for these opportunities to improve your skills and stay knowledgeable.

Get a Landlord-Tenant Attorney

Not all attorneys are alike. This vital resource should specialize in landlord-tenant law. In many areas you need to have an attorney to file an unlawful detainer action after your tenant's three-day notice to pay rent or quit expires because it is just too complicated for an owner-operator to do on his or her own. Develop a relationship with your landlord-tenant attorney because this relationship can save you time and money in the long-run. If you have a question about the best way to approach a difficult situation with a tenant it's better to spend a few hundred dollars on a consultation with your attorney than to make a bad choice on your own and end up in a lawsuit or other disagreement with your tenant that could cost you thousands of dollars.

In many urban areas you'll also have to work with a Department of Building Inspection's division of housing services to make sure your property meets all current codes and is safe for tenants and the public. These government officials are typically assigned to conduct a basic inspection of the common areas of all rental housing every few years as a part of their job to ensure safety and habitability. Frequently, if you and your tenant have a disagreement about how a repair should be completed or whether something needs to be fixed to maintain habitability, your tenant will call the Housing Inspector to do an inspection and settle the issue.

As the owner of the building you are allowed to complete construction projects in your building without hiring a general contractor, though you are required to obtain the necessary permits. I strongly recommend against this practice for all but the most experienced rental property owners. This is not your house where, ostensibly, you're the only person who could be hurt by work you didn't complete correctly. In a rental property your tenants and their families could be injured by poor quality work.

It's absolutely essential that you understand the laws of operating your rental property and commit yourself to following them, just like the rules for driving a car. The more knowledgeable you are about these laws the more confident you'll be and the better your relationships with your tenants will be.

Record Keeping - The Key to Growing Your Portfolio

Precise and thorough record keeping is critical to your success. When you go to buy a building you're going to need good records from the seller to verify that the building has performed as advertised and give you some insights to validate that you could possibly do better. The same goes for your own books. If you're going to approach a bank ten years after you buy the building and they're going to lend you more money you need to have good records that will verify the money you've made. They're most likely going to lend you money based on this prior performance. This is how you grow your business and go from a "second salary" to a third and beyond if you're really ambitious. We're also going to talk briefly about depreciation and some of the tax benefits of being a rental property owner in this section.

Growing Your Portfolio Through Record Keeping

Let's say you find yourself considering investing in your second building after ten years of successfully operating your first. Now's your chance to take back some of the accumulated equity you've earned and use it as a down payment on the next property. Your records are the most important resource you have that will show the bank you've done a good job and the building is worth more now than it was when you bought it. The bank will want to see your tax returns, your rent roll, your income and expense reports and the like, to verify that you've been successful and your building can make your new mortgage payment. Your checkbook register is not enough. You can't just show them that you've got a bunch of cash laying around. You need to be able to pull up a computerized record of how much money was received and how much you spent on a regular basis. I'd recommend getting a good financial software package like QuickBooks to help you make sure that everything is recorded and can be shared easily and cleanly.

Having great records makes the refinancing process so much easier. A successful refinance can allow you to go buy another property that makes cash flow from the beginning. We have come to the point where we are through with the first purchase and we are done with managing for growth. You have done it, you are ready to grow.

Tax Benefits: Write-Offs and Depreciation

Real estate investing has some wonderful tax advantages that make it more profitable than other investments, like your house. For starters, your apartment building is an income-producing investment that provides you with long-term cash flow benefits, your "second salary" and, in most circumstances, equity appreciation over time. Your house only provides you with equity appreciation, meaning that you benefit from its increase in value but not from income production. Another important difference is that your repair and maintenance expenses on your apartment building are tax deductible, whereas the same expenses for your house are not. If you make $100,000 per year in gross income on your apartment building and spend $60,000 on repairs and maintenance your taxable net income is $40,000, not the full $100,000. Essentially, by saving you the cost of taxes your apartment building expenses are discounted by around 30%, the amount you'd pay in taxes if you didn't spend the money.

Another important benefit is that your cash proceeds on a refinance are tax free. If your current mortgage has a balance of $500,000 and you take out a new loan for $750,000, the first $500,000 of your new loan goes to pay off the old loan and the remaining $250,000 goes straight into your pocket. Your loan payment every month might be higher but you're able to use $250,000 in cash that you didn't have before and you still own the building and have access to your "second salary," albeit at a somewhat reduced rate.

Depreciation is another tax benefit that helps to shelter your income, especially in the beginning of your investment cycle. Depreciation is an accounting practice that allows you to divide the purchase price of your property by it's "useful life" (defined by the IRS as 27.5 years for rental property) and shelter that amount of its income from income taxes every year. This allows you to recapture the value of the property as it "wears out" over time.

For example, if you buy your building for $1,000,000 you allocate 85% ($850,000) of the purchase price to the structure and 15% ($150,000) to the land. Structures wear out and land does not. Dividing $850,000 by 27.5 gives an annual depreciation rate of $30,909 per year, meaning that your first $30,909 of income is tax free, ostensibly to allow you to put this money away to rebuilding the property after it's exhausted.

When you first buy the property you are probably going to have a depreciation deduction that is close to your net income so your net income will be tax free. If you have a significantly larger depreciation deduction at the end of your first year, you can use that deduction to shelter your income from other sources, such as your salary at your full-time job.

What's interesting about this practice is that it's a bit ridiculous to assume that a well-built apartment building is going to be "used up" after 27.5 years. Most of the apartment buildings in this city were built more than 27.5 years ago.

They are at least 50 years old. There have been multiple depreciation schedules on them, gone through and exhausted, but the buildings are still standing. Think about these tax benefits as you think about why you are going to invest in an apartment building. You do not get to deduct depreciation when you buy a house.

Harvesting Your Success

Let's say that you've purchased an apartment building and have run it for a number of years efficiently, profitably, and you're very happy with the outcome. You have increased your rents. You have happy tenants. The building is well maintained. Your maintenance issues are minimum. Your monthly costs are minimum and your revenue is quite high or nearing maximum profitability in today's market. Congratulations!

Looking at Your Options

At this juncture there are a few options. They have to do with a next step. If you are happy with the cash flow that the building is generating for you every month and your goal, is to have a certain fixed income and a well maintained building and happy tenants, and if all you wanted and you're happy with your debt that's in place on the building, if you're happy with the loan that you currently have and you can afford it, the one option to do in that case is to stay put and don't sell, and don't refinance. You stay put. You simply stay put. You collect the money every month. You maintain the building and you'll know more or less what you're going to get each month, because as I mentioned, you've approached maximum profitability in today's market. You've done everything you can do to achieve that. You're taking that cash flow every month. You're happy. You put it to bed. You maintain the building. That's that.

Chapter 4: Building Upon Your Success

What do savvy investors do once they achieve that maximum profitability point? I've broken down a few of these time-tested options up into four parts. I'll discuss Refinancing and Selling. I'll cover two refinancing options and two selling options.

Refinancing Options

Refinancing is simply the act of taking your current debt that you have with a lender and replacing that debt with new debt. Because you've achieved higher income on the building and the building is well maintained, the building is worth more and your equity is higher in the building, meaning the asset is just more valuable. A lender will look at that and say "I'm comfortable lending more than the current lender has in place on the building. I am willing to lend up to let's say as a rough number 70% of the new value of the building based on that increased revenue that the building's taking in and the efficiency of that building."

Let's say you bought the building for $700,000 and you currently have $500,000 in debt on the building. The building is now worth a $1,000,000 because of the mindful management you conducted over the years. A lender says "I'll lend you $700,000." You take that $700,000, you pay off $500,000 to the old lender. Now you have $200,000 in tax-free income. Why is it tax-free? This is because it's new debt. It is not income. You have not earned anything. You have not sold anything. You have taken on new debt, so it's tax-free. Obviously there's a cost to that debt in terms of its monthly payment but it is tax-free money. You do not declare it as income.

You can do a couple of things with that $200,000. You can take the money and simply use it for cash if there is something that you want to buy, if you want to put a down payment on a new house, if you want to do a remodeling job, if you want to start a college fund for a child, if you want to take two years off and travel. Whatever it may be, that's your option. Now the only danger–the one concern is does the building support that new debt. You've gone from $500,000 in debt to $700,000 in debt. Does the income that that building generates support that debt? Or are you going to pay that debt down from another source, for your daily job or from the sale of another asset? Who knows? Obviously new debt has new costs so just be aware of that, but it's a wonderful option.

The other approach you can do is once you refinance and you get that $200,000 is you buy another property. That $200,000 can then become the down payment. Let's say you want to buy another million dollar building. You take that

$200,000 and let's say you've also saved another $100,000. you take that 200, you add it to the 100. You have 300,000 now as down payment for a million dollar building and you invest that money into a new building and you start the cycle over again on a new asset just like you had done with the original asset.

Then you simply apply all of the steps that you have performed before to build profitability, increase efficiencies, decrease costs, happy tenants, high income, good building, great investment. You start that cycle again. Refinancing approaches are terrific because they are tax-free way of drawing equity for your building. You're essentially taking cash out of the building and using it for new investments or whatever you may need in your personal life.

If you were to choose instead to sell you're the $1,000,000 building. You'll then have $300,000 in profit. That profit, if you do not a 1031 tax exchange into a new building (I'll go into that process more later in detail) - is taxed as capital gains. 25% to 35% of that money goes to the Federal Government so you are looking at a roughly $75,000 tax bill. That's why I like Refinancing so much.

The advantage with refinancing is you maintain ownership of the building. In a way it's a way of selling the building even though you're not selling it, but you're drawing cash from it, new cash that didn't exist at the time you purchased it, but you've improved it and now that cash does exist so you're utilizing that cash. In a way you can think of it as selling a percentage of the building, although you are paying yourself back. You maintain ownership, which is a great thing. You are now taking on new debt but the building over time but you continue to take advantage of gains down the road from those appreciation and other benefits I mentioned that allow you to increase your cash flow. There's the tax advantages of the depreciation write-off that is probably still active on the building. It's 27.5 years so it depends how long you've owned it. Then you maintain the asset. It's always nice to own property and to be able to do with it as you please and continue to generate income from it.

Sales Options

Now, that concludes the refinance section, and I'd like to talk about the other options, which include selling the building. These options will be split into two parts. Selling the building is not quite as simple as you would think, in that you don't just go off and sell the building and then you get a bunch of money and then you're done. There are implications. The biggest implication in terms of selling a building is capital gains. Having originally paid $700,000 for the property. You now have $500,000 in debt and the property is now worth $1,000,000. You have $300,000 that's exposed to capital gains taxes and you will wipe away that debt. You will no longer receive income from the building so that you can your profits.

When you do not do anything with that money such as buy another property, it's called "cashing out." For a lot of people cashing out is a great option even with this capital gains implication. The reason it's a great option is because sometimes you just need to money. You sell the building for a million. You have $300,000 in capital gains. You pay $75,000 in capital gains. You still have $225,000 of profit that you keep. You earned cash flow on this asset. It appreciated in value. You earned almost 30% or so in profit over time. It was a successful investment and there are other things you would like to do with that cash, any number of things.

Why Sell Your Property?

Why do people sell buildings in this way? Dissolution of a marriage is very common. Dissolution of a partnership is very common. Some people simply do not want to be landlords anymore. They do not like the process of dealing with tenants and maintenance. They've lost their taste for it. They want to do something else. People move and a lot of people do not want to be that far away from such an important asset, that physically far away from such an important asset and do not want to hire a property manager to look after it for them, and sell as a result. There are myriad reasons and all are valid.

That's always an option. Whenever I sell a building for a client I go in and look at the building and I make sure there's no value in the building that should be unlocked before it goes on the market. An important thing about cashing out is that you want to cash out the maximum value, obviously. If there's deferred maintenance issue that should be addressed it's well worth the time and effort to fix those things. If there are things to improve the appearance of the building, make it more attractive, make it a happier place, a nicer place, those things should be done. If there are issues surrounding tenants, difficult tenants, there are ways to remedy or at least alleviate some of the pain from those issues as well.

There are a number of things I look at before someone should sell. They shouldn't just wake up one morning and say "I want to sell the building. Let's put it on the market." It should be a much more strategic process, and with a good apartment broker they should be able to help you do that.

On average, buildings take 60 to 90 days from being on the market to actually closing. When cashing out make sure you put some money aside to be able to pay those capital gains earnings. Talk to a CPA to project how much that will cost. Make sure you do not spend that money or invest it into another source. It's going to become due the next tax cycle – then you can go off into the sunset.

Selling at the Top of the Market

The other option is if let's say you want to sell. Again, you've achieved more or less maximum profitability in today's market. You've taken this asset from a weaker position to a much stronger position. You've completed a cycle in doing that and now you want to sell it, and thus realize those profits, take those profits. It's like selling a stock at its peak vehicle. You have a target that you want it to get to. You got there, sell it, realize those profits but you're still interested in real estate. You still want to be invested in real estate.

Understanding the 1031 Tax Deferred Exchange

The number one channel in this approach is called the 1031 tax deferred exchange. To recap, you purchased your building for $700,000, selling it for $1,000,000. If you take all of that totals $300,000. Actually, the next asset that you buy has to be of equal or greater value in order to shield the whole $300,000, so you buy a property that is worth at least $1,000,000. For example, let's say you have $300,000 in capital gains. You know you have $300,000 in profit. You have $300,000 in cash. You also have $200,000 because remember you bought for $700,000, you currently have $500,000 in debt, so that means you're going to get $500,000 in cash, 300,000 of which is profit subject to capital gains. $200,000 is the money returned to you, the equity you've earned, or your down payment, or whatever it is. It's your money coming back to you.

You have $500,000 and now you say, "I want to take that $500,000 and I want to invest all of that into a property." Now I can get a larger property. I take that $500,000 and say "I can put roughly 30% down on a new property and I want to invest all that $500,000." That means a building more or less worth $1,600,000 is now available to me. I can take all of that money and put it into a property worth $1,600,000. I've turned a $700,000 property now into a $1,600,000 property and I've generated cash flow the whole way.

If you purchase correctly and in the right market and at the right time and at the right price, and that's a good deal, that $1.6 million property should be generating you even more income than the million-dollar building did because you have more rent coming in. That's all in the numbers and that all depends on buying right and buying the right asset.

Relinquished Property

You take all that money. When you sell your property, what's called the relinquished property, that money moves into an escrow account managed by a 1031 exchange management firm. They hold that money until you are ready to purchase your new property, and then the money goes directly from that exchange company to the escrow of the new property. You never touch it. The money never goes to you. That's very important in order to complete a 1031 exchange. You can't ever have the money. You can sell the property, take the money, hold it for three months, and say "Now I want a 1031 exchange." You can't do that. You have to time it, and there's very unique timelines in this process that are important to be aware of.

The 180 Day Clock

The most important timeline is 180 days. The 180 days represents between the time that you sell your property you have to close on the new property in 180 days. You have six months between sale and purchase to go through. There's some other dates in there and timelines that are also important but that's the most important one. That money, again, this whole property goes into a escrow account and you have that time period, that 180 days until you transfer that into a new property.

This is a very popular method and it encourages people to transact and have properties change hands because there's not a capital gains hit. If this program did not exist it would decrease commerce. It would decrease the sale of buildings. Having buildings change hands is a good thing. People invest. New investors come in and they invest in the building. They improve buildings; they find its highest and best use; they create jobs; they are hiring contractors and engineers and foundation experts, roofers, architects to redesign buildings and bring about their highest and best use. The 1031 exchange is a wonderful tool to grow the economy.

Now that we've covered the four typical options you have, the fifth option that I mentioned earlier is staying put, not doing anything– continuing to cash flow the property taking your monthly income and do with that money as you please. The next level of strategic management is refinance and cash out, refinance and investment in another building, sell the building and cash out, or sell the building and investment in another building, another larger building and work towards achieving maximum profitability on that new property as well.

Those are the five options, and what I love doing is sitting down with my clients and discussing these five options and discussing the pros and cons of each of them, because they each have their advantages. It matters so much to people. These assets are hugely important to people's financial futures, their financial well-being, the stability of their families. They're very important decisions to make. They have huge implications and I love sitting down and exploring all the different options and all the different pros and cons, and coming up with a solution that works for them, and helping them achieve their goals.

Let's keep in touch.

We hope that you have found this information helpful and that you have a better sense of what it takes to be a smart apartment investor. Should you be interested to learn more, or have additional questions about buying, managing and leveraging or selling your property, our team is available to you.

For property management questions call (415) 821-3167 or email me, J.J. Panzer, at jj@RMCsf.com For buying or selling questions call (415) 230-8887 or email RMC's Strategic Sales Group Senior Agent, Joshua Silverman at josh@RMCsf.com.

Thank You and Happy Investing!

www.ingramcontent.com/pod-product-compliance
Lightning Source LLC
Chambersburg PA
CBHW060644210326
41520CB00010B/1733